I0210952

www.finishinglinepress.com

Pillow-Stones

poems by

Renée Ruderman

Finishing Line Press
Georgetown, Kentucky

Pillow-Stones

*Dedicated with love and joy
to my grandchildren, Charlie and Ira*

ACKNOWLEDGMENTS

"Delft Pastoral in Six Tiles," Winner Gary Gildner Poetry Prize, *I-70 Review*
"Blackbirds" In *Urge, Poems by Finalists in the 2016 Alexander and Dora Raynes
    Poetry Competition*, judged by Alicia Ostriker—Blue Thread Books, *Jewish
    Currents.*
"Taking Tea, 1938," *Bridges: A Jewish Feminist Journal* 2011
"Overcast," PMS (poemmemoirstory) 2009 (Photograph: FPG/Hulton Archive/
    Getty)
"For Onkel Hans K., 1942," *I-70 Review* 2012
"Mikveh, *"Obama Institute for Transnational American Studies*, Annual Report, 2018,
    Mainz, Germany
"Ode to the Carnival Fountain in Mainz, Germany—," *I-70 Review* 2020
"Home Work," *Homes* Anthology—*Main Street Rag Press* 2015
"Next Door to Letchworth," *Rio Grande Review* 2007
"No Trespassing," *PMS* (poemmemoirstory) 2009
"Thirteen," *Texas Review—Borderlands* 2006
"Dissolve," *I-70 Review*, 2022
"M. Bombardier" *Bridges: A Jewish Feminist Journal* 2007
"Mother's Portrait," In *The American Dream: 40 Poems from the 2013 Alexander and
    Dora Raynes Poetry Competition*—Blue Thread Communications; *Jewish
    Currents*
"Confession," *Writer's Digest*—6th place, *Writer's Digest* Writing Competition, Non-
    Rhyming Poetry 2013
"According to Some," *I-70 Review,* 2021
"Salvation," *I-70 Review*, 2019

Publisher: Leah Huete de Maines
Editor: Christen Kincaid
Cover Art: K. Klaus, 1919
Author Photo: Renée Ruderman
Cover Design: Elizabeth Maines McCleavy

Order online: www.finishinglinepress.com
            also available on amazon.com

Author inquiries and mail orders:
Finishing Line Press
PO Box 1626
Georgetown, Kentucky 40324
USA

Table of Contents

I

Delft Pastoral in Six Tiles

I
Early morning and the tiles are tinted:
the sheep spill into standing sleep;
Each seems intent on its place.
Veined clouds brush sky.
A north wind shoots through the scene.
I sink into the arms of my pillows.

II.
The sheep swell into cobalt blue,
dark water under a wave. They huddle
to pull grass they haven't trampled.
Above them, mottled, is a cluster
of trees, poplars perhaps. They fuse
into smoke wafting south.

III.
The trees have long, thin trunks
as if they had to grow too quickly,
and weather has not been kind to them,
ripping holes in their congregation.
Now I see a shepherd and blurry dog
poke their silhouettes through the grazing.

IV.
The sheep form a reluctant army,
licking the ground before the somnolent march.
The herder waits long enough for prayers,
before he dreams stiff commands; the dog
barks an ear-jangling cadence. A gust
breaks up a batch of clouds.

V.
Twilight and the clouds spread yellow.
The sheep droop in a heavy ring,
their backs fuzzy hillocks, tails flicking.
The shepherd never tires, thinking always
of the remaining fields before shearing time.
A wind makes the trees whine.

VI.
Dust settles on the tiles;
everything melts into blotches.
I cover my eyes with my hands.
This is a scene that must have
a long night, that can only
exist in quick, blue glances.

Blackbirds

(based on a drawing by Kurt Böttcher)

Two blackbirds caw, their beaks open to hasten the sky-bound
flocks toward what's left in the wind-bitten tree. They stretch their
necks to place their sound just below the cumulous cloud—under
which specks of wings accumulate like dark gliders. Another
bird on a lower branch spies the ground, the grass still green,
flower husks holding the promise of seeds. The birds prepare
to fly south, over the Alps from this park near the Bahnhof in
Fürth, where no one walks the curving path into the woods. It's
1920. The Pegnitz River streams under the delicate branches, and
the Great War is over, the next brewing in the valley beyond the
forest. The blackbirds understand about leaving. They do it every
year at the first gust of impossible wind.

Taking Tea, 1938

The servant wheels it in:
the teacart with edges of beveled glass.

On top, the polished silver pot
filmed in steam, embraced by cream, sugar cubes.

The women discuss
their remedies for pains, their plans.

Each sits on a horsehair chair,
armrests bony under lace.

They'll soon have to give up sugar,
and haven't had coffee in weeks.

Each looks toward
the curtained window, but not out.

They want to be somewhere else,
but the teacart is insistent,

like a child tugging to play.
Inside the cart are brötchen,

initialed napkin rings,
tiny forks that once lifted caviar.

Inside the hems of their long kleider.
they have already sewn wedding rings.

Each chin pauses above a teacup
at the sound of a motor spurting, slowing.

Each breath is counted,
blown out like a candle.

Overcast

These photos
you have seen many times:
the bundled women
carrying suitcases,
misshapen bags;
the columns of children
in drooping jackets
carrying small boxes,
the trudge of obedient shoes.

A woman balances
a string-tied valise
on her hatted head
as the procession
flees Paris. She holds
the hand of a boy;
you can see his mouth
is a flat line of trust.
His older brother,
chin tucked into collar,
hoists his elbows like wings.

There's one man
in a fedora walking
toward the city.
Perhaps he'll use
the rifle
strapped to his back.
The naked trees stiffen
their patient branches
at the slow march
as if Brueghel's
silver skating pond
were directly ahead of them,
as if ice will be
the only coming cold.

For Onkel Hans K., 1942

All you are is a face in a photo
with a slicked back shock of blonde,
and eyes, squinting, looking aside.

This would be your last day
on earth. They would shoot
you with the others, but I imagine

you wearing a dark suit
taking long strides into the moist
air from the North Sea.

You smell the fresh bread,
then see the baker's drab awning,
though the window is boarded.

You pay too much for the loaf,
then turn onto the street
where your mother is

in hiding in that always cold,
window-less room,
though the stove feigns warmth.

Maybe you feel chilled
in the dawn wind and wrap
your coat more tightly.

You want to run from them,
alarm ringing your throat;
body a bag of knots,

but they ask for your papers.
You search as if a thief
in your own pockets.

At the Jewish Cemetery in Worms, Germany

Sunlight is sparse here
        as if the gravestones
                might balk at too much.

Shadows slide over the scene
        like weary hands waving
                over the Sabbath candles.

The boughs are empty of song.
        A brisk wind has shooed
                the birds away.

Scattered ash trees dangle
        ropey branches
                brushing passersby.

        The motley headstones
                always waiting
                        to be touched—

        some wear crowns of moss;
                some crumble
                        beneath blue lichen,

        but some tombstones
                daven toward the east,
                        toward the broken wall.

        Hebrew letters
                like scolded skin
                        sink into cracks.

        Pebbles perch on some
                pressing their prayers—
                        stone into stone.

Versteckt
(for my grandfather Gustav)

It might as well be night this afternoon,
and, in the half-light, I find your tallit,
a scroll in a box. I think of you, always
an old man, whose lap I sat in watching

the tin frog hop across your roll-top desk.
You, scarce of hair, played the stock market
under the winsome portrait of your mother.
Your scent was shoe polish, pipe tobacco,

and schnapps in that New York apartment:
too few windows, too much heat,
and the shades drawn over some shame.

There's a photograph of you with my grandmother
gathered under your arm like rolled newspaper.
Her pinched face shows she has already endured
the Turnip Winter. But you? You are stout under

slicked-back hair. You fled Germany after
the Beer Hall Putsch—to Holland where
you were sheltered by a robust Dutch woman.
But Grandmother was versteckt, collar loose

at her throat, writing verses, measuring loneliness
with pen, all while under a thin blanket for years.
I turn on a light, lay the shawl with its blue
thread on my shoulder, offering no prayer.

After the war (at the urging of others) you reunited
with your wife, both of you consigned
to that New York apartment as if
the bomb-strafed sky above Utrecht
had not torn all your vows.

> *Versteckt—hidden; tallit—Jewish prayer shawl; Turnip Winter*
> *1916-17; Putsch—failed coup by Nazis in Munich, 1933*

Mikveh—Speyer, Germany

They could be the stairs to hell, down, down
down the stone steps to the shallow water.
This is where the woman must cleanse her body,
every month, walk down, in robe, toward purity.
She touches the stones that line the walls,
the air passing her like sluggish moth wings.

Shedding robe, she obliges this ritual, knowing
no one will disturb her in the candlelit chamber down
below. She hears the trickling pool where one wall
holds a prayer she will recite in the water.
She will give her nakedness over to purification.
Her hair, unlike Ophelia's, must sink with her body.

She settles in the groundwater, allowing her body
to blend into the moist air, feeling the twinge
of her husband's need. She doesn't feel impure,
but she wants the solitary bathing; she presses down
her long hair, her face, into the tepid water
letting her fingers touch her body in this most walled

off of places. To touch there and there, to break the wall
using the music of her body,
to languish in the holiness of water.
This moment yields a wild wingspread
with which she'll climb the stairs, avoiding down-
drafts, pulling the tangles of her hair, snuffing the pure

white candles in each sconce. She is purely
herself as she alights the passageway, when the walls
open, and the arched doorway presents—sundown.
She widens her eyes, while her body
like a gem reflects the fading light; the clouds are wings
of lace hovering over the mikveh, the enduring water.

Her strides loose footprints and a soft water
in her eyes, on her forehead, pulsing, purifying.
The air tastes of greenery. Now her arms swing
and her limbs sweep her far from the limestone walls.
In the ritual bath she has reclaimed her body.
She departs like Naomi, but she can go down

again, because she loves the water, plain walls.
She pockets purity, knows her body
requires no wings. She will pass her art down.

Ode to the Carnival Fountain in Mainz, Germany—
(An Abecedarian)

Ah ha! Carnival night near the Fastnachts-
Brunnen in the Schillerplatz.
Choose this November darkness for revelry,
Drink from steins among festivalgoers, and
Egos will tangle and flaunt,
Fool, jest, pun, and defy until…
Glass turns to bronze, virtue to vice.
Hop to the hurly-burly of a horn solo, and
Idols smirking atop jesters, hats pointing in a
Jumble of jolly. Three tiers of
Knavery leaning, slacking, and grinning above the
Lubricated below, the lingering crowds of
Mainz on this mischievous Carnival Day.
Niches and mouths dribble, spray water
On each other, and masks, breasts, twist in the
Pandemonium and hullabaloo,
Quipping, quaffing in the brouhaha… but the
Rhine doesn't party with the carousers,
Slips noiselessly like a shadow spirit
Till it bends, bows, and blends into the North Sea,
Used, but splendid with memories,
Views and vows spilled into its span,
Wearing its wilted jewelry, broken flowers,
Xenic cultures, and unused weapons,
Yawning bravely now as the night's
Zest turns to zero.

II.

Home Work

My mother moved paintings, furniture
        late at night in her red robe,
long hair in thin strands down her back;

head tilted like a Modigliani,
        while frames unhinged themselves,
and chair legs marched into new positions.

Her warm milk cooled in the kitchen.
        It was not decoration she was after;
rather stations for her restlessness,

to create a museum of hope, or, at least
        of questions, for when the patrons woke up.
The Cézanne print she'd hung in the hallway

was replaced by a lively Brueghel feast,
        and two chairs from the dining room
made their way to the piano

as if one page turner would sit left,
        one listener on the right. She would have
played a Schubert Lied were it not

for the way the notes rolled upstairs.
        In the morning I lived in a house
not quite my own; night visitors

had rearranged the landscape. But
        I understood the fever of the familiar
and knew that moving

was what she had to do
        to shuffle regrets.
to stage the darkness.

Captive

Sometimes I could not bear
to look into her face
for all the sadness there.

She'd play a Chopin nocturne, not an air.
I'd hear the minor key; more than a trace
sometimes I could not bear.

She'd pace the evening floor to swear
no god could save her from this space
for all the sadness there.

Roses withered without her care;
beetles gnawed a sickly lace
sometimes I could not bear.

Some nights I'd hear her bedroom prayer:
a cry, a plea, no state of grace
for all the sadness there.

She ached for love that she could share
just to ban the pain, a constant mate.
Sometimes I could not bear
her face, for all the sadness there.

The Letchworth Asylum

On groggy gray days
    a black Morris Minor
        rattling with children
            sped like a shot marble

over the broken trellis
    atop the raised sidewalk
        toward the Letchworth thrift shop.

The mother blew dust
    from the shelves of potholders
        the stack of straw brooms
            clowns with sock heads and ankle bells,

while the children strained toward
    the barred windows, heard
        the scrape of metal on linoleum.

At home they wondered
    would the loonies escape
        wend their way toward the family barn

that smelled of hay
    rotting wood and motor oil
        where they played doctor?

What might the crazies see
    through the sifted light?
        a girl laid out on a board
            an examination in progress,

the other children threatening her
    with Letchworth—
        if she made a noise
            if she told another soul.

No Trespassing

In the uncut meadow we were cowboys or Indians.
I was always the scout, nimble and carrot-eating,
vision so good I could spy a jay's feather in the brook's sludge.

The scrawny cowboy-hatted boys sent me ahead
into the woods scrambled with raspberry vines,
rolling in milkweed and the sheen of poison ivy.

With bare feet I crushed mossy groundcover,
hopped granite boulders, brushed droplets off boughs.
Birds accompanied my missions, scouts themselves,

until I stood in the brook, where none could follow my trail;
I could lose the skinned-knee, know-it-alls.
The knee-deep water would drown their messages.

I climbed on a rock, a slippery lookout.
I saw only sunrays spinning through limbs,
not a nodding cowboy hat or dangling holster,

not a whoop or warning whistle carried my name.
I would be a deserted explorer. I'd return with no report,
emerge from among the No Trespassing signs

still seeing the opposite bank: coal clumps spilled
near rusting tracks, and the blackened circles
of campfires left by hobos and men of the night.

Thirteen

Silence befriended this sulky boy
whose shadow jerked along wallpaper,
        whose hands shucked anyone's touch.

Up the attic staircase he trundled, in his arm
a model airplane he would glue together in a dizzying vapor
        as he sat cross-legged under the eaves.

He pieced the gray plastic nose to the fuselage,
snapped the clear cockpit over the seated pilot,
        slid the wet, star decal to the tail wing,

in a fever of low humming
as the turbines shook, sucked air.
        The attic fan spun a giant propeller

and the roof poured out its tarmac.
Then he saw glorious red suns,
        skies hung in mushroom shapes,

his fists punching clouds
into immense wings to sing
        his ripening body and meatless arms.

Dissolve

What to do about her brand-new breasts
at the annual swim party,
not bulges or buds, but plump plums.

Her mother drove her uphill
out of the fields
to the Bedford house

with its shimmering pool,
bobbing plastic tubes,
lawn chairs staring at blue water.

"Girls change together in the foyer,
boys, in the basement,"
directed Mrs. Bedford.

The girl wedged under a staircase
not far enough from the glares
and sniggers of the Bedford twins.

At least the suit flattened the breasts
into two silky slices.
What would the water do?

Sliding in, she watched
the water swell the nylon.
Her chest ballooned.

Once in deeper water
the kids yelled her further in.
She would not swim.

There had to be a way
of stepping out
without her breasts,

exhaling them
to float or be preserved,
spoils for another season.

M. Bombardier

For the small-town high school French teacher
who gave them a language, the girls smirked,

tongues leaping at the roofs of their mouths
a sneer on their lips, "Liberté, Egalité , Fraternité.

Each day he wore the green jacket
flecked with black, they marked him.

After class, the girls followed him
down the hill under a cave of maples,

peered into the remaining light
of his basement apartment.

They watched him pace,
polished shoes glinting.

Their lungs swollen with giggles,
the girls pranced their way home.

Consider what M. Bombardier saw:
the continuous march of white socks,

the parts in the girls' hair as they doodled,
his last flight over the foggy channel.

One day French class cancelled, hall talk
about the gray gunshot in the afternoon.

The girls huddled, lips like chalk,
each walked home through sparser trees

before night pulled the curtains.

Mother's Portrait

My mother peers beyond
the bed and I stretch
into a pink sky morning.
She, too, looks east as if
Berlin were not so long ago.
Her chin tilts above the territory
of sheets below;
there's no one who's
loved her daughter enough:
her terrible tossing, the picked skin,
the skidding teeth.

It's not that Mother's nosy
or a scold there in her golden frame,
or that she's stopped loving the earth
she left long ago.
She's reliving the dark German days
from which she'll escape, and there's
no room for me in that frame, but
soon she'll tug my nightgown,
sketch for me a small boat,
then muss my hair
and there'll be a weedy bank
or a stony point
we'll both go over together.

Confession

I used to check the hymn board
for the songs of the morning,
squinting at the crooked numbers,
passing the Sunday school door.
Outside I sprinted toward the maple limbs
whose sturdy branches waited for me
above the perfume of the lilac bush.
Coloring Joseph's coat couldn't replace
spinning helicopter seeds
or the scraped, sappy knee I licked of blood.

Now, I hurl expletives like a baton twirler,
so, the air swells with witnesses.
I adore a shady patch under twists of pine.
I love the word "blasphemy,"
applaud profanity.
My music is my own, Beatles or Bach.
I don't need back doors or fingers
that interlock to show church, steeple, people.
Nor do I worry that the church bell
will sink me like a sedative.

I still hear the slip and shiver
of the hymnal's pages. The altar is dark—
but something of the sacred, past
the palm fronds I swung like whips,
crosses my lips,
cancels my scorn:
a brittle prayer,
a small candle for justice,
a face bent over psalms,
a bow to thunderclouds and rain.

According to some…

I'm letting myself go.
        A pejorative, of course.

"She's letting herself go.
        Her image is fading;
        her varicose veins protrude;
        her outfits are shabby.
        (See the frayed cuffs!)
She should dye her hair."

Where am I going?
        Past the window for a glance:
            without foundation,
            or slick smile;
        away from snug clothes
        too-high heels, buffed nails,
        seasonal colors.

Yes, I'm letting myself go…
        toward a tipsy life.
        I twirl one aspen leaf
            like a top that
            releases a fan
spreading into a startling geography
        a loose landscape:
        pockets of nightfall
        seams of succulents
        wrinkled weeds
undressed air
buttons that promise to let go.

Salvation

My occasional god   I like to kiss her
      When she's least available,
      Like during an early snow
      Or after too much rain.

She's amenable   I know this because
      She usually says nothing,
      But the air feels clearer,
      My breath lunges deeper.

My occasional god   is never intrusive
      I don't sit and kneel.
      I don't recite ready-made prayers.
      I don't worry when I swear.

My occasional god   appreciates my bursts
      Of language, likening them
      To ongoing planetary mishaps,
      None of which disturb the Milky Way.

My occasional god   does not require crosses
      Or reliquaries, not robes, nor candles.
      Singing, however, she likes,
      But I usually hum.

My occasional god   is a lover
      With no bodily form,
      But great passion.
      We swirl counterclockwise.

My occasional god   could be on a bench
      With what I might call crossed legs
      Listening to crows babble and cackle
      In the leaves above, uttering an occasional sigh.

Walking with my Granddaughter at Crown Hill Park

She's hooded, masked
      in brisk wind.
I'm in gray sneakers;
      the path half-covered
in packed snow.

She's sure-footed, a lynx;
      I am her tracker
      testing each new territory.

We round a bend parallel
      to the Rockies.
The wind shifts
      and its bite takes
      my footing.
"It's only two miles around,"
      she says as I slide
      into her elbow's peak;

then drift onto a winter sidewalk
      in New York City,
      where I knot my arm
      into my grandmother's.

Together, I think we are iron;
      we tell stories
      with trust in
      our sensible shoes,
nodding to the brick corner's
      shock of wind.

The bundle that
       is my granddaughter
       laughs above a slope
       that we weave down
       like a pair of stones,

one sure of earth's hold,
       the other slipping
       through a murmur of pine.

Renée Ruderman is an English Professor Emerita from Metropolitan State University of Denver who has two published books: *Poems from the Rooms Below* and *Certain Losses*, and now *Pillow-Stones*, a number of prizes, numerous publications (See Acknowledgements page), and a black cat. During two sabbaticals she taught poetry classes in the Czech Republic and Germany respectively. She's originally from New York City and loves urban as well as nature-filled environments.

www.ingramcontent.com/pod-product-compliance
Lightning Source LLC
Chambersburg PA
CBHW022056080426
42734CB00009B/1378